What's awake?

Foxes

Louise Spilsbury

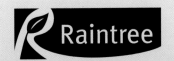

www.raintreepublishers.co.uk
Visit our website to find out more information about **Raintree** books.

To order:
☎ Phone 44 (0) 1865 888112
📄 Send a fax to 44 (0) 1865 314091
💻 Visit the Raintree Bookshop at **raintreepublishers.co.uk** to browse our catalogue and order online.

First published in Great Britain by Raintree, Halley Court, Jordan Hill, Oxford OX2 8EJ, part of Harcourt Education.
Raintree is a registered trademark of Harcourt Education Ltd.

Editorial: Nick Hunter and Diyan Leake
Design: Joanna Sapwell (www.tipani.co.uk) and Michelle Lisseter
Picture Research: Maria Joannou
Production: Lorraine Hicks

Originated by Dot Gradations
Printed and bound in China by South China Printing Company

ISBN 1 844 21352 8
07 06 05 04 03
10 9 8 7 6 5 4 3 2 1

British Library Cataloguing in Publication Data
Spilsbury, Louise
Foxes
599.7'75
A full catalogue record for this book is available from the British Library.

Acknowledgements
The publishers would like to thank the following for permission to reproduce photographs: FLPA pp. **10** (Martin H. Smith), **13** (By Silvestris), **15** (John Hawkins), **18** (Terry Whittaker), **19** (Terry Whittaker); Heather Angel p. **22**; Holt Studios p. **23**; Imagestate p. **4** (First Light), Nature Picture Library p. **7**; NHPA pp. **6** (Manffred Danegger), **8** (Andy Rouse), **9** (David Tomlinson), **17** (Andy Rouse); Oxford Scientific Films pp. **11**, **12** (Michael Leach), **14** (Mark Hamblin); RSPCA Photolibrary pp. **16** (Vanessa Lloyd), **20** (Stuart Harrop), **21** (Colin Seddon); Sylvia Cordaiy Picture Library p. **5**

Cover photograph of a fox, reproduced with permission of Science Photo Library (William Ervin)

Every effort has been made to contact copyright holders of any material reproduced in this book. Any omissions will be rectified in subsequent printings if notice is given to the publishers.

CAUTION: Remind children that it is not a good idea to handle wild animals. Children should wash their hands with soap and water after they touch any animal.

Some words are shown in bold, **like this.** You can find them in the glossary on page 23.

Contents

What's awake?

Some animals are awake when you go to sleep.

Animals that stay awake at night are **nocturnal**.

Foxes are awake at night.

What are foxes?

Foxes are **mammals**.

Mammals have **fur** on their bodies.

Mammals live with their babies.

Mammal babies drink milk from their mother's body.

What do foxes look like?

Foxes have orange-red **fur**.

They have black legs and white fur on their belly.

Foxes have a big bushy tail.

They have large pointed ears and a long **muzzle**.

Where do foxes live?

Some foxes live in woods.

Some live in hills or fields.

Foxes live where they can find food.

Sometimes they live near people.

What do foxes do at night?

Most foxes wake up just after dark.

They hunt for food.

Some foxes hunt all night.

Other foxes only hunt just after dark and before morning.

What do foxes eat?

In the wild, foxes usually eat rabbits, birds and mice.

They sometimes eat plant roots and berries.

In the city, foxes eat these things, too.

They also eat food from dustbins, bird tables or **compost heaps**.

What do foxes sound like?

Foxes can yelp and growl.

They may bark when they are angry.

Foxes call loudly to tell each other where they are.

They open their **muzzle** wide.

How are foxes special?

Foxes can hear very well with their big ears.

They can hear a tiny mouse squeak from far away.

Foxes can live in different places.

They can live near people or in the wild.

Where do foxes go during the day?

In the morning foxes find a safe place.

Then they lie down and go to sleep.

Sometimes foxes hunt during the day.

They do this if they cannot find food at night.

Fox map

muzzle

ears

fur

tail

Glossary

compost heap
pile of old food

fur
hair on an animal's body

hunt
search for and catch other animals
to eat

mammal
animal that has fur on its body and feeds
its babies with milk from its body

muzzle
nose and mouth of an animal such as a
fox or dog

nocturnal
awake at night

roots
the part of a plant that grows
underground

Index

Titles in the What's Awake? series include:

Hardback   1 844 21353 6

Hardback   1 844 21354 4

Hardback   1 844 21352 8

Hardback   1 844 21355 2

Find out about the other titles in this series on our website www.raintreepublishers.co.uk